# Code of Ethics for Nurses

with **Interpretive Statements**

**ANA**
AMERICAN NURSES ASSOCIATION

Silver Spring, Maryland 2015

The American Nurses Association is the only full-service professional organization representing the interests of the nation's 3.4 million registered nurses through its constituent/state nurses associations and its organizational affiliates. ANA advances the nursing profession by fostering high standards of nursing practice, promoting the rights of nurses in the workplace, projecting a positive and realistic view of nursing, and by lobbying the Congress and regulatory agencies on healthcare issues affecting nurses and the public.

**American Nurses Association**
8515 Georgia Avenue, Suite 400
Silver Spring, MD 20910-3492
1-800-274-4ANA
www.Nursingworld.org

**Published by Nursesbooks.org**
The Publishing Program of ANA
www.Nursesbooks.org

Library of Congress Cataloging-in-Publication available on request: copyright@ana.org.

ISBN-13: 978-1-55810-599-7      SAN: 851-3481      08/2019R
First printing: January 2015. Second printing: April 2015. Third printing: August 2016.
Fourth printing: November 2018. Fifth printing: August 2019.

# Contributors and Acknowledgments

This revision of the *Code of Ethics for Nurses with Interpretive Statements* was informed by over 7,800 responses from 2,780 nurses in an online public survey of the 2001 Code. After a revised code was drafted, it was posted for public comment to which more than 1,500 additional responses, representing approximately 1,000 nurses were posted. The contributions of these nurses are gratefully acknowledged.

The revisions were implemented by a steering committee convened to revise the 2001 Code. The members of that committee represented a variety of nursing roles and settings and were drawn from across the United States. The following persons were members of the Steering Committee for the Revision of the Code of Ethics for Nurses with Interpretive Statements:

Margaret Hegge, EdD, RN, FAAN – Chair
Marsha Fowler, PhD, MDiv, MS, RN, FAAN
Dana Bjarnason, PhD, RN, NE-BC
Timothy Godfrey, SJ, DNP, RN, PHCNS-BC
Carla Lee, PhD, APRN-BC, FAAN
Lori Lioce, DNP, FNP-BC, CHSE, FAANP
Margaret Ngai, BSN, RN
Catherine Robichaux, PhD, RN, CNS
Kathryn Schroeter, PhD, RN, CNOR, CNE
Josephine Shije, BSN, RN
Elizabeth Swanson, DNP, MPH, APRN-BC
Mary Tanner, PhD, RN
Elizabeth Thomas, MEd, BS, RN, NCSN, FNASN
Lucia Wocial, PhD, RN
Karen Zanni, MSN, FNP-C

The Steering Committee was staffed by Laurie Badzek, LLM, JD, RN, FAAN, Director of ANA's Center for Ethics and Human Rights (Co-Chair), and Martha Turner, PhD, RN-BC, Assistant Director for ANA's Center for Ethics and Human Rights, who served as content editor, revision coordinator, and co-lead writer. Committee member Marsha Fowler, PhD, MDiv, MS, RN, FAAN, who was named Historian and Code Scholar, served as co-lead writer.

# Contents

## Contents

# Provisions of the Code of Ethics for Nurses with Interpretive Statements

**Provision 1** | The nurse practices with compassion and respect for the inherent dignity, worth, and unique attributes of every person.

**Provision 2** | The nurse's primary commitment is to the patient, whether an individual, family, group, community, or population.

**Provision 3** | The nurse promotes, advocates for, and protects the rights, health, and safety of the patient.

**Provision 4** | The nurse has authority, accountability, and responsibility for nursing practice; makes decisions; and takes action consistent with the obligation to promote health and to provide optimal care.

**Provision 5** | The nurse owes the same duties to self as to others, including the responsibility to promote health and safety, preserve wholeness of character and integrity, maintain competence, and continue personal and professional growth.

**Provision 6** | The nurse, through individual and collective effort, establishes, maintains, and improves the ethical environment of the work setting and conditions of employment that are conducive to safe, quality health care.

**Provision 7** | The nurse, in all roles and settings, advances the profession through research and scholarly inquiry, professional standards development, and the generation of both nursing and health policy.

**Provision 8** | The nurse collaborates with other health professionals and the public to protect human rights, promote health diplomacy, and reduce health disparities.

**Provision 9** | The profession of nursing, collectively through its professional organizations, must articulate nursing values, maintain the integrity of the profession, and integrate principles of social justice into nursing and health policy.

# Preface

The *Code of Ethics for Nurses with Interpretive Statements* (the Code) establishes the ethical standard for the profession and provides a guide for nurses to use in ethical analysis and decision-making. The Code is nonnegotiable in any setting. It may be revised or amended only by formal processes established by the American Nurses Association (ANA). The Code arises from the long, distinguished, and enduring moral tradition of modern nursing in the United States. It is foundational to nursing theory, practice, and praxis in its expression of the values, virtues, and obligations that shape, guide, and inform nursing as a profession.

Nursing encompasses the protection, promotion, and restoration of health and well-being; the prevention of illness and injury; and the alleviation of suffering, in the care of individuals, families, groups, communities, and populations. All of this is reflected, in part, in nursing's persisting commitment both to the welfare of the sick, injured, and vulnerable in society and to social justice. Nurses act to change those aspects of social structures that detract from health and well-being.

Individuals who become nurses, as well as the professional organizations that represent them, are expected not only to adhere to the values, moral norms, and ideals of the profession but also to embrace them as a part of what it means to be a nurse. The ethical tradition of nursing is self-reflective, enduring, and distinctive. A code of ethics for the nursing profession makes explicit the primary obligations, values, and ideals of the profession. In fact, it informs every aspect of the nurse's life.

The *Code of Ethics for Nurses with Interpretive Statements* serves the following purposes:

- It is a succinct statement of the ethical values, obligations, duties, and professional ideals of nurses individually and collectively.
- It is the profession's non-negotiable ethical standard.
- It is an expression of nursing's own understanding of its commitment to society.

Statements that describe activities and attributes of nurses in this code of ethics and its interpretive statements are to be understood as normative or prescriptive statements expressing expectations of ethical behavior. The Code also expresses the ethical *ideals* of the nursing profession and is, thus, both normative and aspirational. Although this Code articulates the ethical obligations of all nurses, it does not predetermine how those obligations must be met. In some instances nurses meet those obligations individually; in other instances a nurse will support other nurses in their execution of those obligations; at other times those obligations can only and will only be met collectively. ANA's *Code of Ethics for Nurses with Interpretive Statements* addresses individual as well as collective nursing intentions and actions; it requires each nurse to demonstrate ethical competence in professional life.

Society recognizes that nurses serve those seeking health as well as those responding to illness. Nurses educate students, staff, and others in healthcare facilities. They also educate within communities, organizations, and broader populations. The term *practice* refers to the actions of the nurse in any role or setting, whether paid or as a volunteer, including direct care provider, advanced practice registered nurse, care coordinator, educator, administrator, researcher, policy developer, or other forms of nursing practice. Thus, the values and obligations expressed in this edition of the Code apply to nurses in all roles, in all forms of practice, and in all settings.

ANA's *Code of Ethics for Nurses with Interpretive Statements* is a dynamic document. As nursing and its social context change, the Code must also change. The Code consists of two components: the provisions and the accompanying interpretive statements. The provisions themselves are broad and noncontextual statements of the obligations of nurses. The interpretive statements provide additional, more specific, guidance in the application of this obligation to current nursing practice. Consequently, the interpretive statements are subject to more frequent revision than are the provisions—approximately every decade—while the provisions may endure for much longer without substantive revision.

Additional ethical guidance and details can be found in the position and policy statements of the ANA or its constituent member associations and affiliate organizations that address clinical, research, administrative, educational, public policy, or global and environmental health issues.

The origins of the *Code of Ethics for Nurses with Interpretive Statements* reach back to the late 1800s in the foundation of ANA, the early ethics literature of modern nursing, and the first nursing code of ethics, which was formally adopted by ANA in 1950. In the 65 years since the adoption of that first professional ethics code, nursing has developed as its art, science, and practice have evolved, as society itself has changed, and as awareness of the nature and determinants of global health has grown. The *Code of Ethics for Nurses with Interpretive Statements* is a reflection of the proud ethical heritage of nursing and a guide for all nurses now and into the future.

# Introduction

In any work that serves the whole of the profession, choices of terminology must be made that are intelligible to the whole community, are as inclusive as possible, and yet remain as concise as possible. For the profession of nursing, the first such choice is the term *patient* versus *client.* The term *patient* has ancient roots in *suffering;* for millennia the term has also connoted one who undergoes medical treatment. Yet, not all who are recipients of nursing care are either suffering or receiving medical treatment. The root of *client* implies one who listens, leans upon, or follows another. It connotes a more advisory relationship, often associated with consultation or business.

Thus, nursing serves both patients and clients. Additionally, the patients and clients can be individuals, families, communities, or populations. Recently, following a consumerist movement in the United States, some have preferred *consumer* to either *patient* or *client.* In this revision of the American Nurses Association's (ANA's) *Code of Ethics for Nurses with Interpretive Statements* (the Code), as in the past revision, ANA decided to retain the more common, recognized, and historic term *patient* as representative of the category of all who are recipients of nursing care. Thus, the term *patient* refers to clients or consumers of health care as well as to individuals or groups.

A decision was also made about the words *ethical* and *moral.* Both are neutral and categorical. That is—similar to *physical, financial,* or *historical*—they refer to a category, a type of reflection, or a behavior. They do not connote a rightness or goodness of that behavior.

Within the field of ethics, a technical distinction is made between *ethics* and *morality. Morality* is used to refer to what would be called personal values, character, or conduct of individuals or groups within communities and societies. *Ethics* refers to the formal study of that morality from a wide range of perspectives including semantic, logical, analytic, epistemological, and normative. Thus, ethics is a branch of philosophy or theology in which one reflects on morality. For this reason, the study of ethics is often called *moral philosophy* or *moral theology*. Fundamentally, ethics is a theoretical and reflective domain of human knowledge that addresses issues and questions about morality in human choices, actions, character, and ends.

As a field of study, ethics is often divided into metaethics, normative ethics, and applied ethics. *Metaethics* is the domain that studies the nature of ethics and moral reasoning. It would ask questions such as "Is there always an element of self-interest in moral behavior?" and "Why be good?" *Normative ethics* addresses the questions of the *ought*, the four fundamental terms of which are *right* and *wrong*, *good* and *evil*. That is, normative ethics addresses what is *right* and *wrong* in human action (what we *ought* to *do*); what is *good* and *evil* in human character (what we *ought* to *be*); and *good* or *evil* in the ends that we *ought* to seek.

*Applied ethics* wrestles with questions of right, wrong, good, and evil in a specific realm of human action, such as nursing, business, or law. It would ask questions such as "Is it ever morally right to deceive a research subject?" or "What is a 'good nurse' in a moral sense?" or "Are health, dignity, and well-being intrinsic or instrumental ends that nursing seeks?" All of these aspects of ethics are found in the nursing literature. However, the fundamental concern of a code of ethics for nursing is to provide normative, applied moral guidance for nurses in terms of what they ought to do, be, and seek.

Some terms used in ethics are ancient such as *virtue* and *evil*, yet they remain in common use today within the field of ethics. Other terms, such as *ethics* and *morality*, are often—even among professional ethicists—used imprecisely or interchangeably because they are commonly understood or because common linguistic use prevails. For example, one might speak of a person as lacking a "moral compass" or as having "low morals." Another example is the broader public use of the term *ethical*. Ethics is a category that refers to ethical or nonethical behavior: either a behavior is relevant to the category of ethics, or it is not. Here, the term *unethical* has no meaning, although it is commonly used in lectures and discussions—even by professional ethicists—to mean *morally blameworthy*; that is, *wrong*. The terms *should* and *must* are often substituted for the more precise normative ethical term *ought*. *Ought* indicates a moral imperative. *Must* expresses an obligation, duty, necessity, or compulsion, although not an intrinsically moral one. Likewise, *should* expresses an obligation or expediency that is not necessarily a moral imperative.

The English language continues to evolve, and the once firm and clearly understood distinctions between *may* and *can*; *will* and *shall*; and *ought, should,* and *must* have faded in daily language and have come to be used interchangeably in both speech or writing, except in rare instances in which the nuance is essential to an argument. To aid the reader in understanding the terms used, this revision of ANA's *Code of Ethics for Nurses with Interpretive Statements* will, for the first time, include a glossary of terms that are found within the Code.

This revision also includes another innovation: links to foundational and supplemental documents. The links to this material are available on ANA's Ethics webpage. These documents are limited to works judged by the Steering Committee as having both timely and timeless value. Nursing's ethics holds many values and obligations in common with international nursing and health communities. For example, the *Millennium Development Goals* of the United Nations, the World Medical Association's *Declaration of Helsinki* about research involving human subjects, and the International Council of Nurses' *Code of Ethics for Nurses* are documents that are both historically and contemporaneously important to U.S. nurses and nursing's ethics.

The afterword from the 2001 Code has been included and updated to reflect the 2010–2014 revision process. This Introduction, another new component of this revision, was added to provide a general orientation to the terminology and the structure of this document.

The nine provisions of the 2001 Code have been retained with some minor revisions that amplify their inclusivity of nursing's roles, settings, and concerns. Together, the nine provisions contain an intrinsic relational motif: nurse-to-patient, nurse-to-nurse, nurse-to-self, nurse-to-others, nurse-to-profession, nurse-to-society, and nursing-to-society, relations that are both national and global. The first three provisions describe the most fundamental values and commitments of the nurse; the next three address boundaries of duty and loyalty; the final three address aspects of duties beyond individual patient encounters. This revision also retains, for each provision, interpretive statements that provide more specific guidance for practice, are responsive to the contemporary context of nursing, and recognize the larger scope of nursing's concern in relation to health.

It was the intent of the Steering Committee to revise the Code in response to the complexities of modern nursing, to simplify and more clearly articulate the content, to anticipate advances in health care, and to incorporate aids that would make it richer, more accessible, and easier to use.

—Steering Committee for the Revision of the
*Code of Ethics for Nurses with Interpretive Statements*
September 2014

# Provision 1

The nurse practices with compassion and respect for the inherent dignity, worth, and unique attributes of every person.

## 1.1 Respect for Human Dignity

A fundamental principle that underlies all nursing practice is respect for the inherent dignity, worth, unique attributes, and human rights of all individuals. The need for and right to health care is universal, transcending all individual differences. Nurses consider the needs and respect the values of each person in every professional relationship and setting; they provide leadership in the development and implementation of changes in public and health policies that support this duty.

## 1.2 Relationships with Patients

Nurses establish relationships of trust and provide nursing services according to need, setting aside any bias or prejudice. Factors such as culture, value systems, religious or spiritual beliefs, lifestyle, social support system, sexual orientation or gender expression, and primary language are to be considered when planning individual, family and population-centered care. Such considerations must promote health and wellness, address problems, and respect patients' or clients' decisions. Respect for patient decisions does not require that the nurse agree with or support all patient choices. When patient choices are risky or self-destructive, nurses have an obligation to address the behavior and to offer opportunities and resources to modify the behavior or to eradicate the risk.

## 1.3 The Nature of Health

Nurses respect the dignity and rights of all human beings regardless of the factors contributing to the person's health status. The worth of a person is not affected by illness, ability, socioeconomic status, functional status, or proximity to death. The nursing process is shaped by unique patient preferences, needs, values, and choices. Respect is extended to all who require and receive nursing care in the promotion of health, prevention of illness and injury, restoration of health, alleviation of pain and suffering, or provision of supportive care.

Optimal nursing care enables the patient to live with as much physical, emotional, social, and religious or spiritual well-being as possible and reflects the patient's own values. Supportive care is particularly important at the end of life in order to prevent and alleviate the cascade of symptoms and suffering that are commonly associated with dying. Support is extended to the family and to significant others and is directed toward meeting needs comprehensively across the continuum of care.

Nurses are leaders who actively participate in assuring the responsible and appropriate use of interventions in order to optimize the health and well-being of those in their care. This includes acting to minimize unwarranted, unwanted, or unnecessary medical treatment and patient suffering. Such treatment must be avoided, and conversations about advance care plans throughout multiple clinical encounters helps to make this possible. Nurses are leaders who collaborate in altering systemic structures that have a negative influence on individual and community health.

## 1.4 The Right to Self-Determination

Respect for human dignity requires the recognition of specific patient rights, in particular, the right to self-determination. Patients have the moral and legal right to determine what will be done with and to their own person; to be given accurate, complete, and understandable information in a manner that facilitates an informed decision; and to be assisted with weighing the benefits, burdens, and available options in their treatment, including the choice of no treatment. They also have the right to accept, refuse, or terminate treatment without deceit, undue influence, duress, coercion, or prejudice, and to be given necessary support throughout the decision-making and treatment process. Such support includes the opportunity to make decisions with family and significant others and to obtain advice from expert, knowledgeable nurses, and other health professionals.

Nurses have an obligation to be familiar with and to understand the moral and legal rights of patients. Nurses preserve, protect, and support those rights by assessing the patient's understanding of the information presented and explaining the implications of all potential decisions. When the patient lacks capacity to make a decision, a formally designated surrogate should be consulted. The role of the surrogate is to make decisions as the patient would, based upon the patient's previously expressed wishes and known values. In the absence of an appropriate surrogate decision-maker, decisions should be made in the best interests of the patient, considering the patient's personal values to the extent that they are known.

Nurses include patients or surrogate decision-makers in discussions, provide referrals to other resources as indicated, identify options, and address problems in the decision-making process. Support of patient autonomy also includes respect for the patient's method of decision-making and recognition that different cultures have different beliefs and understandings of health, autonomy, privacy and confidentiality, and relationships, as well as varied practices of decision-making. Nurses should, for example, affirm and respect patient values and decision-making processes that are culturally hierarchical or communal.

The importance of carefully considered decisions regarding resuscitation status, withholding and withdrawing life-sustaining therapies, foregoing nutrition and hydration, palliative care, and advance directives is widely recognized. Nurses assist patients as necessary with these decisions. Nurses should promote advance care planning conversations and must be knowledgeable about the benefits and limitations of various advance directive documents. The nurse should provide interventions to relieve pain and other symptoms in the dying patient consistent with palliative care practice standards and may not act with the sole intent to end life. Nurses have invaluable experience, knowledge, and insight into effective and compassionate care at the end of life and should actively engage in related research, scholarship, education, practice, and policy development.

Individuals are interdependent members of their communities. Nurses recognize situations in which the right to self-determination may be outweighed or limited by the rights, health, and welfare of others, particularly in public health. The limitation of individual rights must always be considered a serious departure from the standard of care, justified only when there are no less-restrictive means available to preserve the rights of others, meet the demands of law, and protect the public's health.

## 1.5 Relationships with Colleagues and Others

Respect for persons extends to all individuals with whom the nurse interacts. Nurses maintain professional, respectful, and caring relationships with colleagues and are committed to fair treatment, transparency, integrity-preserving compromise, and the best resolution of conflicts. Nurses function in many roles and settings, including direct care provider, care coordinator, administrator, educator, policy maker, researcher, and consultant.

The nurse creates an ethical environment and culture of civility and kindness, treating colleagues, coworkers, employees, students, and others with dignity and respect. This standard of conduct includes an affirmative duty to act to prevent harm. Disregard for the effects of one's actions on others, bullying, harassment, intimidation, manipulation, threats, or violence are always morally unacceptable behaviors. Nurses value the distinctive contribution of individuals or groups as they seek to achieve safe, quality patient outcomes in all settings. Additionally, they collaborate to meet the shared goals of providing compassionate, transparent, and effective health services.

# Provision 2

The nurse's primary commitment is to the patient, whether an individual, family, group, community, or population.

## 2.1 Primacy of the Patient's Interests

The nurse's primary commitment is to the recipients of nursing and healthcare services—patient or client—whether individuals, families, groups, communities, or populations. Each plan of care must reflect the fundamental commitment of nursing to the uniqueness, worth, and dignity of the patient. Nurses provide patients with opportunities to participate in planning and implementing care and support that are acceptable to the patient. Honest discussions about available resources, treatment options, and capacity for self-care are essential. Addressing patient interests requires recognition of the patient's place within the family and other relationships. When the patient's wishes are in conflict with those of others, nurses help to resolve the conflict. Where conflict persists, the nurse's commitment remains to the identified patient.

## 2.2 Conflict of Interest for Nurses

Nurses may experience conflict arising from competing loyalties in the workplace, including conflicting expectations from patients, families, physicians, colleagues, healthcare organizations, and health plans. Nurses must examine the conflicts arising between their own personal and professional values, the values and interests of others who are also responsible for patient care and healthcare decisions, and perhaps even the values and interests of the patients themselves. Nurses address such conflicts in ways that ensure patient safety and that promote the patient's best interests while preserving the professional integrity of the nurse and supporting interprofessional collaboration.

Conflicts of interest may arise in any domain of nursing activity, including direct care, administration, education, consultation, policy development, and research. Nurses in all roles must identify and, whenever possible, avoid conflicts of interest. Nurses who bill for services and nurse executives with budgetary responsibilities must be especially aware of the potential for conflicts of interest. Healthcare financing and delivery systems may create conflict between economic self-interest and professional integrity. Bonuses, sanctions, and incentives tied to financial targets may present such conflict. Any perceived or actual conflict of interest should be disclosed to all relevant parties and, if indicated, nurses should withdraw, without prejudice, from further participation.

## 2.3 Collaboration

The complexity of health care requires collaborative effort that has the strong support and active participation of all health professions. Nurses should foster collaborative planning to provide safe, high-quality, patient-centered health care. Nurses are responsible for articulating, representing, and preserving the scope of nursing practice, and the unique contributions of nursing to patient care. The relationship between nursing and other health professions also needs to be clearly articulated, represented, and preserved.

Collaboration intrinsically requires mutual trust, recognition, respect, transparency, shared decision-making, and open communication among all who share concern and responsibility for health outcomes. Nurses ensure that all relevant persons, as moral agents, participate in patient care decisions. Patients do not always know what questions to ask or may be limited by a number of factors, including language or health literacy. Nurses facilitate informed decision-making by assisting patients to secure the information that they need to make choices consistent with their own values.

Collaboration within nursing is essential to address the health of patients and the public effectively. Although nurses who are engaged in nonclinical roles (e.g., educators, administrators, policy-makers, consultants, or researchers) are not primarily involved in direct patient care, they collaborate to provide high-quality care through the influence and direction of direct care providers. In this sense, nurses in all roles are interdependent and share a responsibility for outcomes in nursing care and for maintaining nursing's primary commitment to the patient.

## 2.4 Professional Boundaries

The work of nursing is inherently personal. Within their professional role, nurses recognize and maintain appropriate personal relationship boundaries. Nurse–patient and nurse–colleague relationships have as their foundation the promotion, protection, and restoration of health and the alleviation of pain and suffering. Nurse–patient relationships are therapeutic in nature but can also test the boundaries of professionalism. Accepting gifts from patients is generally not appropriate; factors to consider include the intent, the value, the nature, and the timing of the gift, as well as the patient's own cultural norms. When a gift is offered, facility policy should be followed. The intimate nature of nursing care and the involvement of nurses in important and sometimes highly stressful life events may contribute to the risk of boundary violations. Dating and sexually intimate relationships with patients are always prohibited.

Boundary violations can also occur in professional colleague relationships. In all communications and actions, nurses are responsible for maintaining professional boundaries. They should seek the assistance of peers or supervisors in managing or removing themselves from difficult situations.

# Provision 3

The nurse promotes, advocates for, and protects
the rights, health, and safety of the patient.

## 3.1 Protection of the Rights of Privacy and Confidentiality

The need for health care does not justify unwanted, unnecessary,
or unwarranted intrusion into a person's life. Privacy is the right to
control access to, and disclosure or nondisclosure of, information
pertaining to oneself and to control the circumstances, timing, and
extent to which information may be disclosed. Nurses safeguard the
right to privacy for individuals, families, and communities. The nurse
advocates for an environment that provides sufficient physical privacy,
including privacy for discussions of a personal nature. Nurses also
participate in the development and maintenance of policies and
practices that protect both personal and clinical information at
institutional and societal levels.

Confidentiality pertains to the nondisclosure of personal information
that has been communicated within the nurse–patient relationship.
Central to that relationship is an element of trust and an expectation
that personal information will not be divulged without consent. The
nurse has a duty to maintain confidentiality of all patient information,
both personal and clinical in the work setting and off duty in all venues,
including social media or any other means of communication. Because
of rapidly evolving communication technology and the porous nature of
social media, nurses must maintain vigilance regarding postings, images,
recordings, or commentary that intentionally or unintentionally
breaches their obligation to maintain and protect patients' rights to
privacy and confidentiality. The patient's well-being could be
jeopardized, and the fundamental trust between patient and nurse could
be damaged by unauthorized access to data or by the inappropriate or
unwanted disclosure of identifiable information.

Patient rights are the primary factors in any decisions concerning personal information, whether from or about the patient. These rights of privacy and confidentiality pertain to all information in any manner that is communicated or transmitted. Nurses are responsible for providing accurate, relevant data to members of the healthcare team and others who have a need to know. The duty to maintain confidentiality is not absolute and may be limited, as necessary, to protect the patient or other parties, or by law or regulation such as mandated reporting for safety or public health reasons.

Information used for purposes of continuity of care, education, peer review, professional practice evaluation, third-party payments, and other quality improvement or risk management mechanisms may be disclosed only under defined policies, mandates, or protocols. These written guidelines must ensure that the rights, safety, and well-being of the patient remain protected. Information disclosed should be directly relevant to a specific responsibility or a task being performed. When using electronic communications or working with electronic health records, nurses should make every effort to maintain data security.

## 3.2 Protection of Human Participants in Research

Stemming from the principle of respect for autonomy, respect for persons, and respect for self-determination, individuals have the right to choose whether or not to participate in research as a human subject. Participants or legal surrogates must receive sufficient and materially relevant information to make informed decisions and to understand that they have the right to decline to participate or to withdraw at any time without fear of adverse consequences or reprisal.

Information needed for informed consent includes the nature of participation; potential risks and benefits; available alternatives to taking part in the study; disclosure of incidental findings; return of research results; and an explanation of how the data will be used, managed, and protected. Those details must be communicated in a manner that is comprehensible to the patient or a legally authorized representative. Prior to initiation, all research proposals must be approved by a formally constituted and qualified institutional review board to ensure participant protection and the ethical integrity of the research.

Nurses should be aware of the special concerns raised by research involving vulnerable groups, including children, cognitively impaired persons, economically or educationally disadvantaged persons, fetuses, older adults, patients, pregnant women, prisoners, and underserved populations. The nurse who directs or engages in research activities in any capacity should be fully informed about the qualifications of the principal investigator, the rights and obligations of all those involved in the particular research study, and the ethical conduct of research in general. Nurses have a duty to question and, if necessary, to report to appropriate oversight bodies any researcher who violates participants' rights or is involved in research that is ethically questionable, as well as to advocate for participants who wish to decline to participate or to withdraw from a study before completion.

## 3.3 Performance Standards and Review Mechanisms

Inherent in professional nursing is a process of education and formation. That process involves the ongoing acquisition and development of the knowledge, skills, dispositions, practice experiences, commitment, relational maturity, and personal integrity essential for professional practice. Nurse educators, whether in academics or direct care settings, must ensure that basic competence and commitment to professional standards exist prior to entry into practice.

Similarly, nurse managers and executives must ensure that nurses have the knowledge, skills, and dispositions to perform professional responsibilities that require preparation beyond the basic academic programs. This is in full recognition of the relationship of nurse competencies, performance standards, review mechanisms, and educational preparation to patient safety and care outcomes. In this way, nurses—individually, collectively, and as a profession—are responsible and accountable for nursing practice and professional behavior.

## 3.4 Professional Responsibility in Promoting a Culture of Safety

Nurses must participate in the development, implementation, and review of and adherence to policies that promote patient health and safety, reduce errors and waste, and establish and sustain a culture of safety. When errors or near misses occur, nurses must follow institutional guidelines in reporting such events to the appropriate authority and must ensure responsible disclosure of errors to patients. Nurses must establish processes to investigate causes of errors or near misses and to address system factors that may have been contributory. While ensuring that nurses are held accountable for individual practice, errors should be corrected or remediated, and disciplinary action taken only if warranted. When error occurs, whether it is one's own or that of a coworker, nurses may neither participate in, nor condone through silence, any attempts to conceal the error.

Following the appropriate intra-institutional sequence of reporting to authority is critical to maintaining a safe patient care environment. Nurses must use the chain of authority when a problem or issue has grown beyond their problem-solving capacity or their scope of responsibility or authority. Issue reporting in a timely manner promotes a safe environment. Communication should start at the level closest to the event and should proceed to a responsive level as the situation warrants.

## 3.5 Protection of Patient Health and Safety by Acting on Questionable Practice

Nurses must be alert to and must take appropriate action in all instances of incompetent, unethical, illegal, or impaired practice or actions that place the rights or best interests of the patient in jeopardy. To function effectively, nurses must be knowledgeable about ANA's *Code of Ethics for Nurses with Interpretive Statements*; standards of practice for the profession; relevant federal, state, and local laws and regulations; and the employing organization's policies and procedures.

When nurses become aware of inappropriate or questionable practice, the concern must be expressed to the person involved, focusing on the patient's best interests as well as on the integrity of nursing practice. When practices in the healthcare delivery system or organization threaten the welfare of the patient, nurses should express their concern to the responsible manager or administrator or, if indicated, to an appropriate higher authority within the institution or agency or to an appropriate external authority.

When incompetent, unethical, illegal, or impaired practice is not corrected and continues to jeopardize patient well-being and safety, nurses must report the problem to appropriate external authorities such as practice committees of professional organizations, licensing boards, and regulatory or quality assurance agencies. Some situations are sufficiently egregious as to warrant the notification and involvement of all such groups and/or law enforcement.

Nurses should use established processes for reporting and handling questionable practices. All nurses have a responsibility to assist whistleblowers who identify potentially questionable practices that are factually supported in order to reduce the risk of reprisal against the reporting nurse. State nurses' associations should be prepared to provide their members with advice and support in the development and evaluation of such processes and reporting procedures. Factual documentation and accurate reporting are essential for all such actions. When a nurse chooses to engage in the act of responsible reporting about situations that are perceived as unethical, incompetent, illegal, or impaired, the professional organization has a responsibility to protect the practice of nurses who choose to report their concerns through formal channels. Reporting questionable practice, even when done appropriately, may present substantial risk to the nurse; however, such risk does not eliminate the obligation to address threats to patient safety.

## 3.6 Patient Protection and Impaired Practice

Nurses must protect the patient, the public, and the profession from potential harm when practice appears to be impaired. The nurse's duty is to take action to protect patients and to ensure that the impaired individual receives assistance. This process begins with consulting supervisory personnel, followed by approaching the individual in a clear and supportive manner and by helping the individual access appropriate resources. The nurse should extend compassion and caring to colleagues throughout the processes of identification, remediation, and recovery. Care must also be taken in identifying any impairment in one's own practice and in seeking immediate assistance.

Nurses must follow policies of the employing organization, guidelines outlined by the profession, and relevant laws to assist colleagues whose job performance may be adversely affected by mental or physical illness, fatigue, substance abuse, or personal circumstances. In instances of impaired practice, nurses within all professional relationships must advocate for appropriate assistance, treatment, and access to fair institutional and legal processes. Advocacy includes supporting the return to practice of individuals who have sought assistance and, after recovery, are ready to resume professional duties.

If impaired practice poses a threat or danger to patients, self, or others, regardless of whether the individual has sought help, a nurse must report the practice to persons authorized to address the problem. Nurses who report those whose job performance creates risk should be protected from retaliation or other negative consequences. If workplace policies for the protection of impaired nurses do not exist or are inappropriate—that is, they deny the nurse who is reported access to due legal process or they demand resignation— nurses may obtain guidance from professional associations, state peer assistance programs, employee assistance programs, or similar resources.

# Provision 4

The nurse has authority, accountability, and responsibility for nursing practice; makes decisions; and takes action consistent with the obligation to promote health and to provide optimal care.

## 4.1 Authority, Accountability, and Responsibility

Nurses bear primary responsibility for the nursing care that their patients and clients receive and are accountable for their own practice. Nursing practice includes independent direct nursing care activities; care as ordered by an authorized healthcare provider; care coordination; evaluation of interventions; delegation of nursing interventions; and other responsibilities such as teaching, research, and administration. In every role, nurses have vested authority, and are accountable and responsible for the quality of their practice. Additionally, nurses must always comply with and adhere to state nurse practice acts, regulations, standards of care, and ANA's *Code of Ethics for Nurses with Interpretive Statements*.

Given the context of increased complexity, development of evidence, and changing patterns in healthcare delivery, the scope of nursing practice continues to evolve. Nurses must exercise judgment in accepting responsibilities, seeking consultation, and assigning activities to others who provide nursing care. Where advanced practice registered nurses (APRNs) have prescriptive authority, these are not acts of delegation. Both the APRN issuing the order and the nurse accepting the order are responsible for the judgments made and are accountable for the actions taken.

## 4.2 Accountability for Nursing Judgments, Decisions, and Actions

To be accountable, nurses follow a code of ethical conduct that includes moral principles such as fidelity, loyalty, veracity, beneficence, and respect for the dignity, worth, and self-determination of patients, as well as adhering to the scope and standards of nursing practice. Nurses in all roles are accountable for decisions made and actions taken in the course of nursing practice. Systems and technologies that assist in clinical practice are adjunct to, not replacements for, the nurse's knowledge and skill. Therefore, nurses are accountable for their practice even in instances of system or technology failure.

## 4.3 Responsibility for Nursing Judgments, Decisions, and Actions

Nurses are always accountable for their judgments, decisions, and actions: however, in some circumstances, responsibility may be borne by both the nurse and the institution. Nurses accept or reject specific role demands and assignments based on their education, knowledge, competence, and experience, as well as their assessment of the level of risk for patient safety. Nurses in administration, education, policy, and research also have obligations to the recipients of nursing care. Although their relationships with patients are less direct, in assuming the responsibilities of a particular role, nurses not in direct care share responsibility for the care provided by those whom they supervise and teach. Nurses must not engage in practices prohibited by law or delegate activities to others that are prohibited by their state nurse practice acts or those practice acts of other healthcare providers.

Nurses have a responsibility to define, implement, and maintain standards of professional practice. Nurses must plan, establish, implement, and evaluate review mechanisms to safeguard patients, nurses, colleagues, and the environment. These safeguards include peer review processes, staffing plans, credentialing processes, and quality improvement and research initiatives. Nurses must bring forward difficult issues related to patient care and/or institutional constraints upon ethical practice for discussion and review. The nurse acts to promote inclusion of appropriate individuals in all ethical deliberation. Nurse executives are responsible for ensuring that nurses have access to and inclusion on organizational committees and in decision-making processes that affect the ethics, quality, and safety of patient care. Nurses who participate in those committees and decision-making processes are obligated to actively engage in, and contribute to, the dialogue and decisions made.

Nurses are responsible for assessing their own competence. When the needs of the patient are beyond the qualifications or competencies of the nurse, that nurse must seek consultation and collaboration from qualified nurses, other health professionals, or other appropriate resources. Educational resources should be provided by agencies or organizations and used by nurses to maintain and advance competence. Nurse educators in any setting should collaborate with their students to assess learning needs, to develop learning outcomes, to provide appropriate learning resources, and to evaluate teaching effectiveness.

## 4.4 Assignment and Delegation of Nursing Activities or Tasks

Nurses are accountable and responsible for the assignment or delegation of nursing activities. Such assignment or delegation must be consistent with state practice acts, organizational policy, and nursing standards of practice.

Nurses must make reasonable effort to assess individual competence when delegating selected nursing activities. This assessment includes the evaluation of the knowledge, skill, and experience of the individual to whom the care is assigned or delegated; the complexity of the tasks; and the nursing care needs of the patient.

Nurses are responsible for monitoring the activities and evaluating the quality and outcomes of the care provided by other healthcare workers to whom they have assigned or delegated tasks. Nurses may not delegate responsibilities such as assessment and evaluation; they may delegate selected interventions according to state nurse practice acts. Nurses must not knowingly assign or delegate to any member of the nursing team a task for which that person is not prepared or qualified. Employer policies or directives do not relieve the nurse of responsibility for making assignment or delegation decisions.

Nurses in management and administration have a particular responsibility to provide a safe environment that supports and facilitates appropriate assignment and delegation. This environment includes orientation and skill development; licensure, certification, continuing education, and competency verification; adequate and flexible staffing; and policies that protect both the patient and the nurse from inappropriate assignment or delegation of nursing responsibilities, activities, or tasks. Nurses in management or administration should facilitate open communication with healthcare personnel allowing them, without fear of reprisal, to express concerns or even to refuse an assignment for which they do not possess the requisite skill.

Nurses functioning in educator or preceptor roles share responsibility and accountability for the care provided by students when they make clinical assignments. It is imperative that the knowledge and skill of the nurse or nursing student be sufficient to provide the assigned nursing care under appropriate supervision.

# Provision 5

The nurse owes the same duties to self as to others, including the responsibility to promote health and safety, preserve wholeness of character and integrity, maintain competence, and continue personal and professional growth.

## 5.1 Duties to Self and Others

Moral respect accords moral worth and dignity to all human beings regardless of their personal attributes or life situation. Such respect extends to oneself as well: the same duties that we owe to others we owe to ourselves. Self-regarding duties primarily concern oneself and include promotion of health and safety, preservation of wholeness of character and integrity, maintenance of competence, and continuation of personal and professional growth.

## 5.2 Promotion of Personal Health, Safety, and Well-Being

As professionals who assess, intervene, evaluate, protect, promote, advocate, educate, and conduct research for the health and safety of others and society, nurses have a duty to take the same care for their own health and safety. Nurses should model the same health maintenance and health promotion measures that they teach and research, obtain health care when needed, and avoid taking unnecessary risks to health or safety in the course of their professional and personal activities. Fatigue and compassion fatigue affect a nurse's professional performance and personal life. To mitigate these effects, nurses should eat a healthy diet, exercise, get sufficient rest, maintain family and personal relationships, engage in adequate leisure and recreational activities, and attend to spiritual or religious needs. These activities and satisfying work must be held in balance to promote and maintain their own health and well-being. Nurses in all roles should seek this balance, and it is the responsibility of nurse leaders to foster this balance within their organizations.

## 5.3 Preservation of Wholeness of Character

Nurses have both personal and professional identities that are integrated and that embrace the values of the profession, merging them with personal values. Authentic expression of one's own moral point of view is a duty to self. Sound ethical decision-making requires the respectful and open exchange of views among all those with relevant interests. Nurses must work to foster a community of moral discourse. As moral agents, nurses are an important part of that community and have a responsibility to express moral perspectives, especially when such perspectives are integral to the situation, whether or not those perspectives are shared by others and whether or not they might prevail.

Wholeness of character pertains to all professional relationships with patients or clients. When nurses are asked for a personal opinion, they are generally free to express an informed personal opinion as long as this maintains appropriate professional and moral boundaries and preserves the voluntariness or free will of the patient. Nurses must be aware of the potential for undue influence attached to their professional role. Nurses assist others to clarify values in reaching informed decisions, always avoiding coercion, manipulation, and unintended influence. When nurses care for those whose health condition, attributes, lifestyle, or situations are stigmatized, or encounter a conflict with their own personal beliefs, nurses must render compassionate, respectful and competent care.

## 5.4 Preservation of Integrity

Personal integrity is an aspect of wholeness of character that requires reflection and discernment; its maintenance is a self-regarding duty. Nurses may face threats to their integrity in any healthcare environment. Such threats may include requests or requirements to deceive patients, to withhold information, to falsify records, or to misrepresent research aims. Verbal and other forms of abuse by patients, family members, or coworkers are also threats; nurses must be treated with respect and need never tolerate abuse.

In some settings, expectations that nurses will make decisions or take actions that are inconsistent with nursing ideals and values, or that are in direct violation of this *Code of Ethics for Nurses with Interpretive Statements*, may occur. Nurses have a right and a duty to act according to their personal and professional values and to accept compromise only if reaching a compromise preserves the nurse's moral integrity and does not jeopardize the dignity or well-being of the nurse or others. Compromises that preserve integrity can be difficult to achieve but are more likely to be accomplished where there is an open forum for moral discourse and a safe environment of mutual respect.

When nurses are placed in circumstances that exceed moral limits or that violate moral standards in any nursing practice setting, they must express to the appropriate authority their conscientious objection to participating in these situations. When a particular decision or action is morally objectionable to the nurse, whether intrinsically so or because it may jeopardize a specific patient, family, community, or population, or when it may jeopardize nursing practice, the nurse is justified in refusing to participate on moral grounds. Conscience-based refusals to participate exclude personal preference, prejudice, bias, convenience, or arbitrariness.

Acts of conscientious objection may be acts of moral courage and may not insulate nurses from formal or informal consequences. Nurses who decide not to participate on the grounds of conscientious objection must communicate this decision in a timely and appropriate manner. Such refusal should be made known as soon as possible, in advance and in time for alternate arrangements to be made for patient care. Nurse executives should ensure the availabilty of policies that address conscientious objection. Nurses are obliged to provide for patient safety, to avoid patient abandonment, and to withdraw only when assured that nursing care is available to the patient.

When the integrity of nurses is compromised by patterns of institutional behavior or professional practice, thereby eroding the ethical environment and resulting in moral distress, nurses have an obligation to express their concern or conscientious objection individually or collectively to the appropriate authority or committee. Nurse administrators must respond to concerns and work to resolve them in a way that preserves the integrity of the nurses. They must seek to change enduring activities or expectations in the practice setting that are morally objectionable.

## 5.5 Maintenance of Competence and Continuation of Professional Growth

Competence is a self-regarding duty. It affects not only the quality of care rendered but also one's self-respect, self-esteem, and the meaningfulness of work. Nurses must maintain competence and strive for excellence in their nursing practice, whatever the role or setting. Nurses are responsible for developing criteria for evaluation of practice and for using those criteria in both peer and self-assessments. To achieve the highest standards, nurses must routinely evaluate their own performance and participate in substantive peer review.

Professional growth requires a commitment to lifelong learning. Such learning includes continuing education and self-study, networking with professional colleagues, self-study, professional reading, achieving specialty certification, and seeking advanced degrees. Nurses must continue to learn about new concepts, issues, concerns, controversies, and healthcare ethics relevant to the current and evolving scope and standards of nursing practice.

## 5.6 Continuation of Personal Growth

Nursing care addresses the whole person as an integrated being; nurses should also apply this principle to themselves. Professional and personal growth reciprocate and interact. Activities that broaden nurses' understanding of the world and of themselves affect their understanding of patients; those that increase and broaden nurses' understanding of nursing's science and art, values, ethics, and policies also affect nurses' self-understanding. Nurses are encouraged to read broadly, continue life-long learning, engage in personal study, seek financial security, participate in a wide range of social advocacy and civic activities, and pursue leisure and recreational activities.

# Provision 6

The nurse, through individual and collective effort, establishes, maintains, and improves the ethical environment of the work setting and conditions of employment that are conducive to safe, quality health care.

## 6.1 The Environment and Moral Virtue

Virtues are universal, learned, and habituated attributes of moral character that predispose persons to meet their moral obligations; that is, *to do* what is right. There is a presumption and expectation that we will commonly see virtues such as integrity, respect, moderation, and industry in all those whom we encounter. Virtues are what we are *to be* and make for a morally "good person." Certain particular attributes of moral character might not be expected of everyone but are expected of nurses. These include knowledge, skill, wisdom, patience, compassion, honesty, altruism, and courage. These attributes describe what the nurse is to be as a morally "good nurse." Additionally, virtues are necessary for the affirmation and promotion of the values of human dignity, well-being, respect, health, independence, and other ends that nursing seeks.

For virtues to develop and be operative, they must be supported by a moral milieu that enables them to flourish. Nurses must create, maintain, and contribute to morally good environments that enable nurses to be virtuous. Such a moral milieu fosters mutual caring, communication, dignity, generosity, kindness, moral equality, prudence, respect, and transparency. These virtues apply to all nurses, colleagues, patients, or others.

## 6.2 The Environment and Ethical Obligation

Virtues focus on what is *good* and *bad* in regard to whom we are *to be* as moral persons; obligations focus on what is *right and wrong* or what we are *to do* as moral agents. Obligations are often specified in terms of principles such as beneficence or doing good; nonmaleficence or doing no harm; justice or treating people fairly; reparations, or making amends for harm; fidelity, and respect for persons. Nurses, in all roles, must create a culture of excellence and maintain practice environments that support nurses and others in the fulfillment of their ethical obligations.

Environmental factors contribute to working conditions and include but are not limited to: clear policies and procedures that set out professional ethical expectations for nurses; uniform knowledge of the Code and associated ethical position statements. Peer pressure can also shape moral expectations within a work group. Many factors contribute to a practice environment that can either present barriers or foster ethical practice and professional fulfillment. These include compensation systems, disciplinary procedures, ethics committees and consulting services, grievance mechanisms that prevent reprisal, health and safety initiatives, organizational processes and structures, performance standards, policies addressing discrimination and incivility position descriptions, and more. Environments constructed for the equitable, fair, and just treatment of all reflect the values of the profession and nurture excellent nursing practice.

## 6.3 Responsibility for the Healthcare Environment

Nurses are responsible for contributing to a moral environment that demands respectful interactions among colleagues, mutual peer support, and open identification of difficult issues, which includes ongoing professional development of staff in ethical problem solving. Nurse executives have a particular responsibility to assure that employees are treated fairly and justly, and that nurses are involved in decisions related to their practice and working conditions. Unsafe or inappropriate activities or practices must not be condoned or allowed to persist. Organizational changes are difficult to achieve and require persistent, often collective efforts over time. Participation in collective and inter-professional efforts for workplace advocacy to address conditions of employment is appropriate. Agreements reached through such actions must be consistent with the nursing profession's standards of practice and the *Code of Ethics for Nurses with Interpretive Statements*.

Nurses should address concerns about the healthcare environment through appropriate channels and/or regulatory or accrediting bodies. After repeated efforts to bring about change, nurses have a duty to resign from healthcare facilities, agencies, or institutions where there are sustained patterns of violation of patient's rights, where nurses are required to compromise standards of practice or personal integrity, or where the administration is unresponsive to nurses' expressions of concern. Following resignation, reasonable efforts to address violations should continue. The needs of patients may never be used to obligate nurses to remain in persistently morally unacceptable work environments. By remaining in such an environment, even if from financial necessity, nurses risk becoming complicit in ethically unacceptable practices and may suffer adverse personal and professional consequences.

The workplace must be a morally good environment to ensure ongoing safe, quality patient care and professional satisfaction for nurses and to minimize and address moral distress, strain, and dissonance. Through professional organizations, nurses can help to secure the just economic and general welfare of nurses, safe practice environments, and a balance of interests. These organizations advocate for nurses by supporting legislation; publishing position statements; maintaining standards of practice; and monitoring social, professional, and healthcare changes.

# Provision 7

The nurse, in all roles and settings, advances the profession through research and scholarly inquiry, professional standards development, and the generation of both nursing and health policy.

## 7.1 Contributions through Research and Scholarly Inquiry

All nurses must participate in the advancement of the profession through knowledge development, evaluation, dissemination, and application to practice. Knowledge development relies chiefly, though not exclusively, upon research and scholarly inquiry. Nurses engage in scholarly inquiry in order to expand the body of knowledge that forms and advances the theory and practice of the discipline in all its spheres. Nurse researchers test existing and generate new nursing knowledge. Nursing knowledge draws from and contributes to corresponding sciences and humanities.

Nurse researchers may involve human participants in their research, as individuals, families, groups, communities, or populations. In such cases, nursing research conforms to national and international ethical standards for the conduct of research employing human participants. Community consultation can help to ensure enhanced protection, enhanced benefits, legitimacy, and shared responsibility for members of communities during all phases of the research process. Additionally, when research is conducted with the use of animals, all appropriate ethical standards are observed.

Nurses take care to ensure that research is soundly constructed, significant, worthwhile, and in conformity with ethical standards including review by an Institutional Review Board prior to initiation. Dissemination of research findings, regardless of results, is an essential part of respect for the participants. Knowledge development also occurs through the process of scholarly inquiry, clinical and educational innovation, and interprofessional collaboration. Dissemination of findings is fundamental to ongoing disciplinary discourse and knowledge development.

Nurses remain committed to patients/participants throughout the continuum of care and during their participation in research. Whether the nurse is data collector, investigator, member of an institutional review board, or care provider, the patients' rights and autonomy must be honored and respected. Patients'/participants' welfare may never be sacrificed for research ends.

Nurse executives and administrators should develop the structure and foster the processes that create an organizational climate and infrastructure conducive to scholarly inquiry. In addition to teaching research methods, nurse educators should teach the moral standards that guide the profession in the conduct and dissemination of its research. Research utilization and evidence informed practice are expected of all nurses.

## 7.2 Contributions through Developing, Maintaining, and Implementing Professional Practice Standards

Practice standards must be developed by nurses and grounded in nursing's ethical commitments and developing body of knowledge. These standards must also reflect nursing's responsibility to society. Nursing identifies its own scope of practice as informed, specified, or directed by state and federal law and regulation, by relevant societal values, and by ANA's *Code of Ethics for Nurses with Interpretive Statements* and other foundational documents.

Nurse executives establish, maintain, and promote conditions of employment that enable nurses to practice according to accepted standards. Professional autonomy and self-regulation are necessary for implementing nursing standards and guidelines and for assuring quality care.

Nurse educators promote and maintain optimal standards of education and practice in every setting where learning activities occur. Academic educators must also seek to ensure that all their graduates possess the knowledge, skills, and moral dispositions that are essential to nursing.

## 7.3 Contributions through Nursing and Health Policy Development

Nurses must lead, serve, and mentor on institutional or agency policy committees within the practice setting. They must also participate as advocates or as elected or appointed representatives in civic activities related to health care through local, regional, state, national, or global initiatives.

Nurse educators have a particular responsibility to foster and develop students' commitment to the full scope of practice, to professional and civic values, and to informed perspectives on nursing and healthcare policy. Nurse executives and administrators must foster institutional or agency policies that reinforce a work environment committed to promoting evidence informed practice and to supporting nurses' ethical integrity and professionalism. Nurse researchers and scholars must contribute to the body of knowledge by translating science; supporting evidence informed nursing practice; and advancing effective, ethical healthcare policies, environments, and a balance of patient–nurse interests.

# Provision 8

The nurse collaborates with other health professionals and the public to protect human rights, promote health diplomacy, and reduce health disparities.

## 8.1 Health Is a Universal Right

The nursing profession holds that health is a universal human right. Therefore, the need for nursing is universal. As the World Health Organization states: "…the highest attainable standard of health is a fundamental right of every human being." This right has economic, political, social, and cultural dimensions. It includes: access to health care, emergency care, and trauma care; basic sanitation; education concerning the prevention, treatment, and control of prevailing health problems; food security; immunizations; injury prevention; prevention and control of locally endemic diseases and vectors; public education concerning health promotion and maintenance; potable water; and reproductive health care. This affirmation of health as a fundamental, universal human right is held in common with the United Nations, the International Council of Nurses, and many human rights treaties.

## 8.2 Collaboration for Health, Human Rights, and Health Diplomacy

All nurses commit to advancing health, welfare, and safety. This nursing commitment reflects the intent to achieve and sustain health as a means to the common good so that individuals and communities worldwide can develop to their fullest potential and live with dignity. Ethics, human rights, and nursing converge as a formidable instrument for social justice and health diplomacy that can be amplified by collaboration with other health professionals. Nurses understand that the lived experiences of inequality, poverty, and social marginalization contribute to the deterioration of health globally.

Nurses must address the context of health, including social determinants of health such as poverty, access to clean water and clean air, sanitation, human rights violations, hunger, nutritionally sound food, education, safe medications, and healthcare disparities. Nurses must lead collaborative partnerships to develop effective public health legislation, policies, projects, and programs that promote and restore health, prevent illness, and alleviate suffering.

Such partnerships must raise health diplomacy to parity with other international concerns such as commerce, treaties, and warfare. Human rights must be diligently protected and promoted and may be interfered with only when necessary and in ways that are proportionate and in accord with international standards. Examples might include communicable disease reporting, helmet laws, immunization requirements, mandatory reporting of abuse, quarantine, and smoking bans.

## 8.3 Obligation to Advance Health and Human Rights and Reduce Disparities

Advances in technology, genetics, and environmental science require robust responses from nurses working together with other health professionals for creative solutions and innovative approaches that are ethical, respectful of human rights, and equitable in reducing health disparities. Nurses collaborate with others to change unjust structures and processes that affect both individuals and communities. Structural, social, and institutional inequalities and disparities exacerbate the incidence and burden of illness, trauma, suffering, and premature death.

Through community organizations and groups, nurses educate the public; facilitate informed choice; identify conditions and circumstances that contribute to illness, injury, and disease; foster healthy life styles; and participate in institutional and legislative efforts to protect and promote health. Nurses collaborate to address barriers to health—poverty homelessness, unsafe living conditions, abuse and violence, and lack of access—by engaging in open discussion, education, public debate, and legislative action. Nurses must recognize that health care is provided to culturally diverse populations in this country and across the globe. Nurses should collaborate to create a moral milieu that is sensitive to diverse cultural values and practices.

## 8.4 Collaboration for Human Rights in Complex, Extreme, or Extraordinary Practice Settings

Nurses must be mindful of competing moral claims—that is, conflicting values or obligations—and must bring attention to human rights violations in all settings and contexts. Of grave concern to nurses are genocide, the global feminization of poverty, abuse, rape as an instrument of war, hate crimes, human trafficking, the oppression or exploitation of migrant workers, and all such human rights violations. The nursing profession must respond when these violations are encountered. Human rights may be jeopardized in extraordinary contexts related to fields of battle, pandemics, political turmoil, regional conflicts, environmental catastrophes or disasters where nurses must necessarily practice in extreme settings, under altered standards of care. Nurses must always stress human rights protection with particular attention to preserving the human rights of vulnerable groups such as the poor, the homeless, the elderly, the mentally ill, prisoners, refugees, women, children, and socially stigmatized groups.

All actions and omissions risk unintended consequences with implications for human rights. Thus, nurses must engage in discernment, carefully assessing their intentions, reflectively weighing all possible options and rationales, and formulating clear moral justifications for their actions. Only in extreme emergencies and under exceptional conditions, whether due to forces of nature or to human action, may nurses subordinate human rights concerns to other considerations. This subordination may occur when there is both an increase in the number of ill, injured, or at-risk patients and a decrease in access to customary resources and healthcare personnel.

A utilitarian framework usually guides decisions and actions with special emphasis on transparency, protection of the public, proportional restriction of individual liberty, and fair stewardship of resources. Conforming to international emergency management standards and collaborating with public health officials and members of the healthcare team are essential throughout the event.

# Provision 9

The profession of nursing, collectively through its professional organizations, must articulate nursing values, maintain the integrity of the profession, and integrate principles of social justice into nursing and health policy.

## 9.1 Articulation and Assertion of Values

Individual nurses are represented by their professional associations and organizations. These groups give united voice to the profession. It is the responsibility of a profession collectively to communicate, affirm, and promote shared values both within the profession and to the public. It is essential that the profession engage in discourse that supports ongoing self-reflection, critical self-analysis, and evaluation. The language that is chosen evokes the shared meaning of nursing, as well as its values and ideals, as it interprets and explains the place and role of nursing in society. The profession's organizations communicate to the public the values that nursing considers central to the promotion or restoration of health, the prevention of illness and injury, and the alleviation of pain and suffering. Through its professional organizations, the nursing profession must reaffirm and strengthen nursing values and ideals so that when those values are challenged, adherence is steadfast and unwavering. Acting in solidarity, the ability of the profession to influence social justice and global health is formidable.

## 9.2 Integrity of the Profession

The values and ethics of the profession should be affirmed in all professional and organizational relationships whether local, inter-organizational, or international. Nursing must continually emphasize the values of respect, fairness, and caring within the national and global nursing communities in order to promote health in all sectors of the population. A fundamental responsibility is to promote awareness of and adherence to the codes of ethics for nurses (the American Nurses Association and the International Council of Nurses and others). Balanced policies and practices regarding access to nursing education, workforce sustainability, and nurse migration and utilization are requisite to achieving these ends. Together, nurses must bring about the improvement of all facets of nursing, fostering and assisting in the education of professional nurses in developing regions across the globe.

The nursing profession engages in ongoing formal and informal dialogue with society. The covenant between the profession and society is made explicit through the *Code of Ethics for Nurses with Interpretive Statements*, foundational documents, and other published standards of nursing specialty practice; continued development and dissemination of nursing scholarship; rigorous educational requirements for entry into practice, advanced practice, and continued practice including certification and licensure; and commitment to evidence informed practice.

## 9.3 Integrating Social Justice

It is the shared responsibility of professional nursing organizations to speak for nurses collectively in shaping health care and to promulgate change for the improvement of health and health care locally, nationally, and internationally. Nurses must be vigilant and take action to influence leaders, legislators, governmental agencies, non-governmental organizations, and international bodies in all related health affairs to address the social determinants of health. All nurses, through organizations and accrediting bodies involved in nurse formation, education, and development, must firmly anchor students in nursing's professional responsibility to address unjust systems and structures, modeling the profession's commitment to social justice and health through content, clinical and field experiences, and critical thought.

## 9.4 Social Justice in Nursing and Health Policy

The nursing profession must actively participate in solidarity with the global nursing community and health organizations to represent the collective voice of U.S. nurses around the globe. Professional nursing organizations must actively engage in the political process, particularly in addressing legislative and regulatory concerns that most affect—positively and negatively—the public's health and the profession of nursing. Nurses must promote open and honest communication that enables nurses to work in concert, share in scholarship, and advance a nursing agenda for health. Global health, as well as the common good, are ideals that can be realized when all nurses unite their efforts and energies.

Social justice extends beyond human health and well-being to the health and well-being of the natural world. Human life and health are profoundly affected by the state of the natural world that surrounds us. Consistent with Florence Nightingale's historic concerns for environmental influences on health, and with the metaparadigm of nursing, the profession's advocacy for social justice extends to eco-justice. Environmental degradation, aridification, earth resources exploitation, ecosystem destruction, waste, and other environmental assaults disproportionately affect the health of the poor and ultimately affect the health of all humanity. Nursing must also advocate for policies, programs, and practices within the healthcare environment that maintain, sustain, and repair the natural world. As nursing seeks to promote and restore health, prevent illness and injury, and alleviate pain and suffering, it does so within the holistic context of healing the world.

# Afterword

The development of the *Code of Ethics for Nurses with Interpretive Statements* (Code) is a benchmark both for the American Nurses Association (ANA) and for the profession of nursing as a whole.

In its articles of incorporation, ANA set forth the objectives of the Association as follows:

> The object of the Association shall be: to establish and maintain a code of ethics, to the end that the standard of nursing education be elevated; the usefulness, honor, and interests of the nursing profession be promoted; public opinion in regard to duties, responsibilities, and requirements of nurses be enlightened; emulation and concert of action in the profession be stimulated; professional loyalty be fostered, and friendly intercourse between nurses be facilitated. (Alumnae, 1896)

> The first object, then, was the creation and maintenance of a code of ethics for nurses.... The ANA is recognized nationally and internationally as the spokes-organization for nursing in the United States, and as the basis for the US membership in the International Council of Nurses based in Geneva, Switzerland. (Fowler, 2006)

Therefore, the *Code of Ethics for Nurses with Interpretive Statements* serves all U.S. nurses in all settings and in all roles. The Code is also incorporated into the nurse practice acts of a number of states, according it actual regulatory force in those states.

The evolution of the Code dates from Articles of Incorporation of 1896; from 1893, when the "Nightingale Pledge" was written and administered at commencement; and from 1926 and 1940, when tentative codes were suggested but not formally ratified. In 1950, the ANA House of Delegates formally adopted *A Code for Professional Nurses*. It was not accompanied by interpretive statements although the *American Journal of Nursing* subsequently published a series of articles that served this function. There were several subsequent revisions of the Code, approximately every decade, some more substantive than others. The 2001 revision was the first time in 25 years that both the provisions of the Code and the interpretive statements were thoroughly revised.

This 2015 revision is the result of changes made by the Code of Ethics Steering Committee and was informed by 7,800 responses from 2,780 nurses during an online survey of the 2001 Code for public comment. The draft of the revised Code was posted for public comment; more than 1,500 comments from almost 1,000 nurses were received. This 2015 revision of the Code reflects comments from hundreds of nurses across the United States and abroad, multiple drafts, review by the ANA Ethics Advisory Board, and approval by the ANA Board of Directors.

The ethical tradition manifested in every iteration of the Code is self-reflective, enduring, and distinctive. That is, the Code steadfastly supports nurses across all settings and in all roles. The Code is particularly useful at the beginning of the 21st century because it reiterates the fundamental values and commitments of the nurse (Provisions 1–3), identifies the boundaries of duty and loyalty (Provisions 4–6), and describes the duties of the nurse that extend beyond individual patient encounters (Provisions 7–9).

It also addresses the variety of relationships that nurses encounter in the course of their professional duties. The achievement of a true global awareness about the human condition; the sociopolitical, economic, interdependent, environmental context of all humanity; and the universal need for health care are the most important moral challenges of the 21st century. This Code summons nurses to actively meet these challenges.

ANA's *Code of Ethics for Nurses with Interpretive Statements* is the promise that nurses are doing their best to provide care for their patients and their communities and are supporting each other in the process so that all nurses can fulfill their ethical and professional obligations. This Code is an important tool that can be used now as leverage to a better future for nurses, patients, and health care.

# Glossary

**accountability.** To be *answerable* to oneself and others for one's own choices, decisions and actions as measured against a standard such as that established by the *Code of Ethics for Nurses with Interpretive Statements.*

**advocacy.** The act or process of pleading for, supporting, or recommending a cause or course of action. Advocacy may be for persons (whether as an individual, group, population, or society) or for an issue, such as potable water or global health.

**altered standard of care.** Describes how treatment may change in extraordinary circumstances such as natural disasters or warfare. It involves a systematic, uniform, and standardized reprioritization of the allocation of health care.

**altruism.** Disinterested or selfless concern for the well-being or benefit of others as a virtue, principle, and motivation for action.

**autonomy.** Rational self-legislation and self-determination that is grounded in informedness, voluntariness, consent, and rationality.

**beneficence.** The bioethical principle of benefitting others by preventing harm, removing harmful conditions, or affirmatively acting to benefit another or others, often going beyond what is required by law.

**civil rights.** See *rights, civil.*

**collaboration.** Working cooperatively with others, especially in joint intellectual efforts, in a way that includes collegial action and respectful dialog.

**compassion.** An awareness of suffering, tempered with reason, coupled with a desire to relieve the suffering; a virtue combining sympathy, empathy, benevolence, caring, and mercy. Used with the cognitive and psychomotor skills of healing to meet the patient's needs.

**compassion fatigue.** A form of burnout, which results from helping, or desiring to help to relieve the suffering of others. It may appear suddenly and subside more quickly than burnout, which is characterized by emotional exhaustion, depersonalization, and reduced job satisfaction.

**confidentiality.** A right to have one's private, intimate, or secret information kept undisclosed to a third party unless permission is granted for disclosure.

**conflict of interest.** A set of circumstances that creates a risk that the motivation for a nurse's professional judgment or action might be corrupted or unduly influenced by self-interest.

**conscientious objection.** A conscience-based refusal, on moral or religious grounds, to act or participate in an action that falls within the scope of one's practice.

**courage.** The virtue that strengthens one's response in difficult or threatening circumstances or situations.

**culturally sensitive.** Being aware that cultural differences and similarities exist and effect values, learning, preferences, and behavior.

**dispositions, moral.** An intrinsic state of being or qualities of mind or character, in which one has a habit or inclination to act in a specific way morally. Dispositions are shaped by virtues.

**eco-justice.** Contraction of "ecological justice" that links environmental and social justice issues, challenging thereby both humanity's destruction of the earth and the abuse of economic and political power that results in poor people having to suffer disproportionately the effects of environmental damage, particularly those affecting health and well-being.

**environmental degradation.** The deterioration in environmental quality from human activities and processes, such as, improper land use, as well as from natural disasters.

**environmental justice.** A form of justice whose concerns include degradation of agricultural land and food sufficiency; aridification, desertification, water takings, and potable water; ozone layer degradation, deforestation, climate change, and air pollution; habitat loss and ecosystem destruction; industrial waste, sanitation, and nonbiodegradables; and choices of nonreplenishable over replenishable resources. It is also concerned with how various forms of environmental damage in the pursuit of economic self-interest places the heaviest burden upon the poor, forcing them to bear the highest social, environmental, economic, and health costs.

**ethics.** The branch of philosophy or theology in which one reflects on morality; the formal study of morality from a wide range of perspectives including semantic, logical, analytic, epistemological, normative, and applied.

**evidence informed practice.** In any role or setting, practice that is characterized by combining the best available research; role or practice expertise; applied nursing, research, and healthcare ethics; and clinical or experiential insight. In patient care, it includes patient preferences, cultural backgrounds, and community values. Concepts and elements of evidence based practice are used interchangeably with this term in some contexts.

**fidelity.** The ethical principle that requires loyalty, fairness, truthfulness, advocacy, and dedication in relationships. It includes promise-keeping, truth-telling, and fulfilling commitments.

**health diplomacy.** Prioritizing global health issues and concerns within the context of international diplomacy and practices. Bringing together public health, international affairs, management, law, economics, health, foreign policy, and trade, it focuses on negotiations that shape and manage the global policy environment for health.

**human rights.** See *rights, human.*

**impaired practice.** Functioning poorly or with diminished competence, as evident in changes in work habits, job performance, appearance, or other behaviors that may occur in any role or any setting.

**incompetence.** Lack of possession or failure to exercise that degree of learning, skill, care, and experience ordinarily possessed and exercised by a competent professional.

**integrity.** An internal quality (virtue) within oneself; a cluster of attributes. It manifests externally as honesty and moral consistency, i.e., consistency with one's internal values, convictions, beliefs, knowledge, commitments, and obligations. It requires ongoing self-examination and taking seriously one's life, values, commitments, and so forth.

**interprofessional.** Characterized by practicing professionals from two or more academic disciplines working, learning, or taking action together.

**Just Culture.** An organizational environment that holds individuals accountable for performing duties of avoiding harm, producing outcomes and following policies, procedures or guidelines that: recognizes individuals choose and need to manage human error, at-risk behaviors and reckless behaviors;

recognizes individuals make mistakes and systems fail; learns from mistakes, treats individuals fairly; coaches to avoid risky behaviors; and disciplines reckless or knowingly dangerous behaviors.

**justice.** A bioethical principle with various types or domains of justice, including distributive, retributive, restorative, transitional, intergenerational, and procedural. Bioethics is chiefly concerned with distributive justice. Distributive justice deals with the equitable distribution of social burdens and benefits in society. When this allocation occurs under conditions of scarcity, it raises questions of rationing. The formal principle of justice states that equals shall be treated equally, and un-equals unequally, in proportion to their relevant differences.

**metaparadigm.** An overarching and general statement of a discipline that functions as a framework within which conceptual models develop.

**moral distress.** The condition of knowing the morally right thing to do, but institutional, procedural or social constraints make doing the right thing nearly impossible; threatens core values and moral integrity.

**morality.** Refers to personal values, character, or conduct of individuals or groups within communities and societies; often used interchangeably with *ethics*.

**nonmaleficence.** The bioethical principle that specifies a duty not to inflict harm and balances unavoidable harm with benefits of good achieved.

**nursing.** The protection, promotion, and optimization of health and abilities, prevention of illness and injury, alleviation of suffering through the diagnosis and treatment of human response, and advocacy in the care of individuals, families, communities, and populations.

**organizations.** Groups and associations that affiliate to enhance the work of nurses by promoting unity, engaging in political advocacy, disseminating professional knowledge, and facilitating professional development.

**participants (in research).** Persons taking part in research studies under the direction of an investigator who obtains data through interventions, observations or interaction. Also referred to as *subjects*, they agree to participate without coercion or undue influence through an informed consent process. The Federal Policy for the Protection of Human Subjects or (the "Common Rule"), in CFR 45 part 46 outlines protections and specifies requirements when humans participate in research. Research animals are protected by the Animal Welfare Act (1966), administered by the U.S. Department of Agriculture.

**praxis.** The bridging or coming together of theory and practice; theoretically reflective action.

**principles.** Also known as: ethical principles; moral principles; principles of bioethics. Descriptive and prescriptive (normative) rules that form a general theoretical basis for the analysis and specification of right and wrong in ethical situations or issues, and thus are guides to ethical reasoning and action. Four principles are commonly used in bioethics: respect for autonomy, beneficence, justice, and nonmaleficence. These principles are codified in the Belmont Report of 1979. It is asserted that these principles can be used to some degree across various moral theories.

**respect for autonomy.** The bioethical principle that specifies the duty to respect the autonomous (self-determined) decisions of others. This extends to allowing others to act upon their self-chosen plan in so far as such action does not harm others.

**respect for persons.** The principle that human beings bear inherent, intrinsic, and unconditional worth, in and of themselves, and should be valued as such; that is, all persons should be treated with respect simply because they are persons.

**responsibility.** An obligation to perform required professional activities at a level commensurate with one's education and in compliance with applicable laws and standards; the opportunity or ability to act independently and make decisions without authorization; refers to the blameworthiness or praiseworthiness that one bears for one's conduct or the performance of duties. It is often expressed as liability for one's actions and may be apportioned in degree based on circumstances.

**rights, human; rights, civil.** Human rights, sometimes called *natural rights,* are fundamental freedoms to which each and every human being is entitled by virtue of being a human being. Rights include both positive rights (a right to …) and negative rights (a right to be free from…). All persons have a legal and moral right to human rights. Civil rights are rights that are secured by law of the nation or state. Civil rights or civil liberties are freedoms established by the law of a particular state and applied by that state within its own jurisdiction.

**self-regarding duty.** The principle of duties to self, also called the principle of self-regarding duties, exists when the self is the subject, object, and beneficiary of the duty. Each person is owed the same moral regard as is expected of them toward others.

**social determinants of health.** The conditions in which people are born, grow, live, work, and age. They are shaped by the distribution of money, power, and resources at global, national, and local levels.

**social justice.** A form of justice that engages in social criticism and social change. Its focus is the analysis, critique, and change of social structures, policies, laws, customs, power, and privilege that disadvantage or harm vulnerable social groups through marginalization, exclusion, exploitation, and voicelessness. Among its ends are: a more equitable distribution of social and economic benefits and burdens; greater personal, social, and political dignity; and a deeper moral vision for society. It may refer to a theory, process, or end.

**social media.** Forms of electronic communication such as web sites for social networking and blogging where users create online communities to share information, ideas, personal messages, and other content.

**values.** Core beliefs of desirability, worth, or dignity that guide and motivate attitudes and actions, two of which inform ethics. An intrinsic value is a good that has worth in itself and not as a means to another good. An instrumental value is a good that serves as a means to another good. For example, health is an instrumental value as a means to life satisfaction and social contribution.

**virtue.** A habit of character that predisposes one to do what is right; what we are to *be* as moral agents; habituated, learned. Not to be confused with personality traits.

# Timeline:
## The Evolution of Nursing's Code of Ethics

Whatever the version of the Code, it has always been fundamentally concerned with the principles of doing no harm, of benefiting others, of loyalty, and of truthfulness. As well, the Code has been concerned with social justice and, in later versions, with the changing context of health care, and the autonomy of the patient and the nurse.

**1893** | The "Nightingale Pledge," patterned after medicine's Hippocratic Oath, is understood as the first nursing code of ethics.

**1896** | The Nurses' Associated Alumnae of the United States and Canada (later to become the American Nurses Association), whose first purpose was to establish and maintain a code of ethics.

**1926** | "A Suggested Code" is provisionally adopted and published in the *American Journal of Nursing* (AJN) but is never formally adopted.

**1940** | "A Tentative Code" is published in AJN, but also is never formally adopted.

**1950** | *A Code for Professional Nurses,* in the form of seventeen provisions that are a substantive revision of the "Tentative Code" of 1940, is unanimously accepted by the ANA House of Delegates.

**1956** | *A Code for Professional Nurses* is amended.

**1960** | *A Code for Professional Nurses* is revised.

**1968** | *A Code for Professional Nurses* is substantively revised, condensing the seventeen provisions of the 1960 Code into ten provisions.

**1976** | The *Code of Ethics for Nurses with Interpretive Statements,* a modification of the provisions and interpretive statements, is published as eleven provisions.

**1985** | The *Code of Ethics for Nurses with Interpretive Statements* retains the provisions of the 1976 version and includes revised interpretive statements.

**2001** | The *Code of Ethics for Nurses with Interpretive Statements*, a modification of the eleven 1976 provisions and the 1985 interpretive statements, is accepted as nine provisions by the ANA House of Delegates in July and published in September.

**2014** | The *Code of Ethics for Nurses with Interpretive Statements*, a modification of the nine provisions and interpretive statements of 2001, is approved by the ANA Board of Directors (November).

**2015** | The *Code of Ethics for Nurses with Interpretive Statements* is published (January).

# Index

*Note:* A decimal numeral in parentheses (4.1) indicates an interpretive statement of a given numbered ethical provision (Provision 4).

## A

abuse
  as human rights violation, (8.4), 33
  of nurses, (5.4), 20
access to health care, 31, 32, 33
access to health information, (3.1), 9–10
access to legal processes, 12. *See also* patient protection and impaired practice
accountability for practice
  culture of safety and, (3.4), 11–12
  defined, 41
  for nursing judgments, decisions, and actions, (4.2), 15–16
  (Provision 4), 15–18
actions, nursing
  accountability for, (4.2), 15–16
  assignment and delegation of, (4.4), 17
  responsibility for, (4.3), 16–17
administration as nursing role, viii, (4.1), 15
  conflict of interest in, (2.2), 5
  encouragement scholarly inquiry in, (7.1), 28

policy development in, (7.3), 28–29
preservation of integrity in, (5.4), 21
professional practice standards in, (7.2), 28
responsibility for assignment and delegation in, (4.4), 17
responsibility for patient care in, 5, 16
advance care planning, 3
advanced practice registered nurses (APRNs), viii, 15
advancement of profession (Provision 7), 27–29
  contributions through research and scholarly inquiry, (7.1), 27–28
  nursing and health policy development, (7.3), 28–29
  professional practice standards, (7.2), 28
advocacy, defined, 41
advocacy for nurse, (6.3), 25
advocacy for patient (Provision 3), 9–13
  acting on questionable practice, (3.5), 12–13
  performance standards and reviews and, (3.3), 11

advocacy for patient *(continued)*
  promoting culture of safety, (3.4), 11–12
  protecting rights of privacy and confidentiality, (3.1), 9–10
  protection from impaired practice, (3.6), 13
  protection of research participants, (3.2), 10–11
advocacy for policy, (7.3), 28–29
advocacy for social justice, 36–37
advocacy for workplace changes, (6.2), 24
alleviation of suffering, vii, 2, 7, 32, 35, 37
altered standard of care. *See also* standard of care
  defined, 41
  human rights under, (8.4), 33
altruism
  defined, 41
  of nurse, expectation for, (6.1), 23
American Nurses Association (ANA), 35
  *Code of Ethics for Nurses with Interpretive Statements*, v, vii–ix, 39–40
  objectives of, 39
  position and policy statements of, ix
ANA. *See* American Nurses Association (ANA)
animal research, (7.1), 27
applied ethics, xi
APRNs. *See* advanced practice registered nurses
articulation of values, (9.1), 35
assertion of values, (9.1), 35
authority for practice (Provision 4), 15–18
autonomy
  defined, 41
  patient self-determination and, (1.4), 2–3
  of patients, (7.3), 28

professional, (7.1), 28
of research participants, (3.2), 10–11; (7.1), 27–28
respect for (defined), 45

**B**
Belmont Report, 44
beneficence
  defined, 41
  as ethical obligation, (6.2), 23
bioethical principles, 23, 41, 44, 45
boundaries, professional, (2.4), 7

**C**
character
  preserving wholeness of, (5.3), 20
  virtues and, (6.2), 23
civil rights, 46
client (as term), x
*A Code for Professional Nurses* (1950, 1956, 1960, 1968), 40
*Code of Ethics for Nurses with Interpretive Statements* ("The Code"), v, vii–ix, 39–40
  as benchmark, 39
  ethical traditions in, vii, ix, 40
  evolution of, vii, 39–40, 47–48
  as promise and tool, 40
  purposes of, viii
  relational motif in, xii
  revisions of, vii, viii–ix, 40
  terminology in, x–xii
  timeline of, 47–48
  2001 Code and 2015 Code, xi, 40
  21st-century application of, 40
collaboration
  for advancing health and human rights and reducing disparities, (8.3), 32
  commitment to patient in, (2.3), 6
  defined, 41
  and health as universal right, (8.1), 31
  for health, human rights, and health diplomacy, (8.2), 31–32

for human rights in complex, extreme or extraordinary practice settings, (8.4), 33

interprofessional, 5, 27

need for, self-assessment of competence and, (4.3), 16

nurse educator–student, 16–17

Provision 8 on, 31–33

respect for colleagues and others in, (1.5), 4

colleagues

competence of, and delegation, (4.4), 17

impaired practice by, responsibilities in, 13

professional boundaries with, (2.4), 7

respect for, (1.5), 4

collegial action. *See* collaboration

commitment to patient (Provision 2), 5–7

collaboration and, (2.3), 6

conflict of interest for nurses and, (2.2), 5–6

primacy of patient's interests and, (2.1), 5

professional boundaries and, (2.4), 7

compassion

defined, 41

of nurse, expectation for, (6.1), 23

Provision 1 on, 1–4

compassion fatigue, (5.2), 19

defined, 42

competence. *See also* nursing knowledge and skills

of colleagues in delegation, (4.4), 17

impaired practice *versus,* (3.6), 13

maintenance of, (5.5), 22

of others, and delegation, (4.4), 17

self-assessment of, (4.3), 16–17

complex practice settings, human rights in, (8.4), 33

confidentiality

defined, 42

protecting right to, (3.1), 9–10

conflict of interest for nurses, (2.2), 5–6, 42

conscientious objection, 21, 42

consent, informed, (3.2), 10

consultant role for nurses, viii, 4, 6

consumer (as term), x

context of health, (8.2), 31–32

continuing education, (5.5), 22

courage

defined, 42

of nurse, expectation for, (6.1), 23

cultural sensitivity (culturally sensitive), 32, 42

culture of civility and kindness, 4

culture of excellence, (6.2), 23–24

culture of safety, (3.4), 11–12. *See also* Just Culture

## D

data access, rights of privacy and (3.1), 9, 10

data in research, informed consent and, 10

data security, rights of privacy and (3.1), 10

decision-makers, surrogate, (1.4), 2–3

death and dying, 1, 2, 32

decisions, nursing

accountability for, (4.2), 15–16

responsibility for, (4.3), 16–17

Declaration of Helsinki, xii

delegation

competence of colleagues and, (4.4), 17

judgment and, (4.1), 15

of nursing activities and tasks, (4.4), 17

nursing knowledge and skills and, (4.4), 17

delegation *(continued)*
  responsibilities for patient care and, (4.3), 16–17
dignity and worth of individual
  collaboration for health, human rights, and health diplomacy, (8.2), 31–32
  duties to self, (5.1), 19–22
  health as universal right, (8.1), 31
  nature of health and, (1.3), 1–2
  nurse's relationship with patient and, (1.2), 1
  protection of research participants, (3.2), 10–11, 27–28
  respect for colleagues and others, (1.5), 4
  respect for patient, (1.1), 1
  respect for person, 23, 45
  right to self-determination and, (1.4), 2–3
diplomacy, health
  collaboration for, (8.2), 31–32
  defined, 43
direct care as nursing role, viii, 4, 6
discernment, in extreme practice settings, (8.4), 33
disclosure
  of conflict of interest, (2.2), 6
  of errors, (3.4), 11–12
  of health information, (3.1), 9–10
  of research findings, (3.2), 10–11
disparities, health, obligation to reduce, (8.3), 32
dispositions, moral, 28, 42
diversity, sensitivity to, (8.3), 32
duties to patient. *See* commitment to patient; responsibilities of nurses
duties to self (Provision 5), 19–22
  continuation of personal growth, (5.6), 22
  maintenance of competence and continuation of professional growth, (5.5), 22

preservation of integrity, (5.4), 20–21
preservation of wholeness of character, (5.3), 20
promotion of personal health, safety, and well-being, (5.2), 19

# E

eco-justice, (9.4), 37
  defined, 42
economic and financial issues, 6, 25
education, continuing, (5.5), 22
education as nursing role, viii
  advancement of profession in, (7.3), 28–29
  collaboration with colleagues in, (1.5), 4
  collaboration with students in, (4.3), 16–17
  responsibility for patient care in, 5, 16, 17
  standards in, 11, 28
education of public, viii
electronic health records, rights and privacy and (3.1), 10
emergency management standards, (8.4), 33
employment conditions (Provision 6), 23–25
  environment and ethical obligation, (6.2), 23–24
  environment and moral virtue, (6.1), 23
  professional practice standards and, (7.2), 28
  responsibility for healthcare environment, (6.3), 24–25
end-of-life care, (1.4), 2–3
environment, healthcare. *See also* work setting; workplace
  and culture of safety, (3.4), 11–12
  and delegation of activities and tasks, (4.4), 17
  and ethical obligation, (6.2), 23–24
  and moral virtue, (6.1), 23

health *(continued)*
   social determinants of, 31–32,
     36, 46
   as universal right, (8.1), 31
healthcare environment
   and culture of safety, (3.4), 11–12
   and delegation of activities and
     tasks, (4.4), 17
   and ethical obligation, (6.2), 23–24
   and moral virtue, (6.1), 23
   Provision 6 on, 23–25
   responsibility for, (6.3), 24–25
health diplomacy
   collaboration for, (8.2), 31–32
   defined, 43
health policy
   development of, (7.3), 28–29
   social justice in, (9.4), 36–37
health promotion, self-care in,
   (5.2), 19
health restoration, vii, 2, 7, 32, 35
holistic concept, for healing world,
   (9.4), 37
human dignity *See also* dignity and
   worth of individual
human rights
   collaboration for, (8.2), 31–32
   in complex, extreme or
     extraordinary practice settings,
     (8.4), 33
   defined, 45
   obligation to advance, (8.3), 32
human rights violations, (8.4), 33
human trafficking, (8.4), 33

**I**

ideals, ethical, viii
identity, wholeness of character and,
   (5.3), 20
impaired practice
   advocacy for colleagues in, (3.6), 13
   defined, 43
   protecting patient from, 12, 13

incompetence
   defined, 43
   impaired practice and, (3.6), 13
information, personal and clinical. *See*
   patient information; personal health
   information
information and informed consent, 10
informed consent, (3.2), 10
institutional policies, 28–29
institutional review board, 10, 27–28
integrity
   conflict of interest *versus,* (2.2), 5–6
   defined, 43
   healthcare environment and, 23,
     24–25
   institutional policies and, (7.3), 29
   performance standards and, (3.3), 11
   personal, preservation of, (5.4),
     20–21
   of profession, (9.2), 35–36
   questionable practice *versus,* (3.5),
     12–13
   relationship with colleagues and,
     (1.5), 4
   of research, (3.2), 10
   as virtue, (6.1), 23
International Council of Nurses, xii, 35
international emergency management
   standards, (8.4), 33
interpretative statements, viii–ix. *See
   also individual statements*
interprofessional, defined, 44
interprofessional collaboration, 5,
   24, 27
interventions
   assignment or delegation of, 15, 17
   responsibility for, 2, 15

**J**

judgments, nursing
   accountability for, (4.2), 15–16
   responsibility for, (4.3), 16–17
Just Culture, defined, 43–44

justice
   defined, 45
   as ethical obligation, (6.2), 23
justice, ecological, 37, 42
justice, social
   in nursing and health policy, (9.4),
      36–37
   responsibility for integrating, (9.3), 36

**K**

knowledge development, 11, 27. *See
   also* nursing knowledge and skills

**L**

leadership, 1–2
legal issues
   in impaired practice, 13
   in nursing judgments, decisions, and
      actions, 16
   in privacy and confidentiality, 9–10
   in professional practice, 28
   in questionable practice, 12–13
   in research, 10
   in self-determination, 2–3

**M**

management. *See* administration as
   nursing role
meaningfulness of work, 22
metaethics, xi
metaparadigm
   defined, 45
   of nursing, (9.4), 37
migrant workers, 33
Millennial Developmental Goals, xii
monitoring, of delegated tasks, 17
moral discernment, in extreme
   practice settings, (8.4), 33
moral dispositions
   defined, 42
   standards of education and, 28
moral distress
   defined, 44
   preservation of integrity (5.4), 21

moral environment. *See also*
   healthcare environments
responsibility for (6.3), 24
workplace as, 25
moral integrity, (5.4), 20–21
morality
   defined, 45
   *versus* ethics, x–xi
moral milieu, 23
moral philosophy, xi
moral respect, (5.1), 19
moral theology, xi
moral virtue, environment and, (6.1), 23
morally blameworthy (use of term), x
must (use of term), xi–xii

**N**

natural world, social justice and, (9.4),
   37
near misses. *See* errors
Nightingale, Florence, (9.4), 37
"Nightingale Pledge," 39
nonmaleficence
   defined, 44
   as ethical obligation, (6.2), 23
normative ethics, xi
nurse educators, viii
   advancement of profession, (1.5),
      28–29
   collaboration with colleagues, (2.3),
      4
   collaboration with students, (4.3),
      16–17
   responsibility for patient care, 5,
      16, 17
   standards of education, (7.3), 28
nursing, defined, 45
nursing actions. *See* action, nursing
nursing executives, 11. *See also*
   administration as nursing role
nursing knowledge and skills
   advancement of profession and,
      (7.1), 27–28

nursing knowledge and skills
*(continued)*
  development and maintenance of,
    11, 22, 27
  impaired practice *versus,* (3.6), 13
  self-assessment of, (4.3), 16–17
  task assignment or delegation and,
    (4.4), 17
  technology *versus,* (4.2), 16
  virtues of nurse and, (6.1), 23
nursing managers, 11, 12. *See also*
  administration as nursing role
nursing practice
  activities of, (4.1), 15
  assignment and delegation activities
    or tasks in, (4.4), 17
  defined and roles in, viii
  professional standards for, (7.2), 28
  responsibility for (Provision 4),
    (4.1), 15–18
  scope of, 15, 28–29
  nursing students, 9, 10, 17, 28. *See*
    *also* education as a nursing role

# O

obligations of nurses, vii. *See also*
  responsibilities of nurses
  to advance health and human rights
    and reduce disparities, (8.3), 32
  ethical, environment and, (6.2),
    23–24
  nursing roles and, viii
  to understand patient rights,
    (1.4), 2–3
organizational (institutional) policies,
  28–29
organizations
  defined, 45
  professional. *See* professional
    organizations
ought (use of term), xi–xii

# P

participants (in research)
  defined, 44
  protection of, (3.2), 10–11, 27–28
patient(s)
  defined and terminology for, x
  interests of, primacy of, (2.1), 5
  nurse's relationship with, (1.2), 1
patient information, privacy and
  confidentiality and, (3.1), 9, 10
patient rights
  health as universal right, (8.1), 31
  limitations of, (1.4), 3
  personal health information and
    (3.1), 9, 10
  to privacy and confidentiality, (3.1),
    9–10
  in research participation, (), 27–28
  to self-determination, (1.4), 2–3
peer assistance, 7, 13
peer pressure, (6.2), 24
peer review, 16, 22
performance standards and reviews,
  (3.3), 11
personal health, promotion of, (5.2),
  19
personal health information, privacy
  and confidentiality and, (3.1), 9–10
policies, institutional, 28–29
policy, nursing and health
  development of, (7.3), 28–29
  social justice in, (9.4), 36–37
politics, working for social justice in,
  36–37
poverty, feminization of, (8.4), 33
practice. *See also* nursing practice
  defined, viii
  impaired, 13, 43
practice settings, complex or extreme,
  (8.4), 33
practice standards, (7.2), 28

regulatory issues, 10, 12, 15, 28, 36
relational motifs in *Code of Ethics for Nurses with Interpretive Statements*, xiii
relationships, nurse's
  with client, x
  with colleagues and others, (1.5), 4
  with patients, (1.2), 1
  professional boundaries in, (2.4), 7
reparations (making amends for harm), (6.4), 23
reporting questionable practice, 12–13
research
  advancement of profession through, (7.1), 27–28
  animals used in, (7.1), 27
  vulnerable groups involved in, (3.2), 10–11
research participants
  defined, 45
  protection of, (3.2), 10–11, 27–28
resignation, over unacceptable environment, (6.3), 24–25
respect for autonomy, 45
respect for others (Provision 1), 1–4
  nature of health and, (1.3), 1–2
  nurse's relationships with colleagues and others, (1.5), 4
  nurse's relationships with patients, (1.2), 1
  patient's right to self-determination and, (1.4), 2–3
  protection of research participants, (3.2), 10–11, 27–28
  respect for human dignity, (1.1), 1
respect for persons, 23, 45. *See also* respect for others
respect for self (Provision 5), (5.1), 19–22. *See also* self-respect and development
responsibilities of nurses
  for assignment and delegation of nursing activities and tasks, (4.4), 17

for healthcare environment, (6.3), 24–25
for judgments, decisions, and actions, (4.3), 16–17
for nursing practice (Provision 4), 15–18
nursing roles and, viii
responsibility, defined, 45
responsibility for practice (Provision 4), 15–18
restorative care, vii, 2, 7, 32, 35
review, peer, 16, 22
review mechanisms, (3.3), 11
right(s)
  civil, 45
  human, collaboration for, (8.2), 31–32
  human, defined, 46
  human, in complex, extreme, or extraordinary practice settings, (8.4), 33
  human, obligation to advance, (8.3), 32
  patient. *See* patient rights
  universal, health as, (8.1), 31
right *versus* wrong, xi
risk to nurses
  boundary violations and, (2.4), 7
  reporting impaired practice and, (3.6), 13
  reporting questionable practice and, (3.5), 12–13
  self-care for avoiding, (5.2), 19
  unacceptable work environment and, (6.3), 25
risk to patient
  culture of safety and, (3.3), 11–12
  extreme practice settings and, (8.4), 33
  responsibility for assessing, (4.3), 16
risky behavior, of patients, (1.4), 2

## S

safety
  personal, promotion of, (5.2), 19
  promoting culture of, (3.4), 11–12
scholarly inquiry, advancement of
  profession through, (7.1), 27–28
scope of nursing practice, 15, 28–29
self-assessment of competence, (4.3), 16
self-determination, right to, (1.4), 2–3
self-esteem, (5.5), 22
self-reflection, 20, 35
self-regarding duty. *See also* duties
  to self
  defined, 46
self-regulation, professional, (5.5), 28
self-respect and development
  (Provision 5), 19–22
  continuation of personal growth,
    (5.6), 22
  duties to self and others, (5.1), 19
  maintenance of competence and
    continuation of professional
    growth, (5.5), 22
  preservation of integrity, (5.4),
    20–21
  preservation of wholeness of
    character, (5.3), 20
  promotion of personal health,
    safety, and well-being, (5.2), 19
self-understanding (5.6), 22
should (use of term), xi–xii
skills. *See* nursing knowledge and
  skills
social determinants of health,
  31–32, 36
  defined, 46
social justice
  defined, 44
  in health policy (9.4), 36–37
  nurse's commitment to, vii
  in nursing and health policy, (9.4),
    36–37
  responsibility for integrating, (9.3), 36

social media
  defined, 46
  rights to privacy and confidentiality
    *versus,* (3.1), 9
standard of care, human rights and
  (1.4), 3
standards of nursing practice, 11, 28
subjects, research. *See* research
  participants
suffering, alleviation of, vii, 2, 7, 32,
  35, 37
supportive care, (1.3), 2
surrogate decision-makers, (1.4), 2–3

## T

terminology in ethics, x–xii
timeline of nursing's code of ethics,
  47–48

## U

unethical (misuse of term), xi
United Nations, xii, 31
universal right, health as, (8.1), 31
unwarranted treatment, minimizing,
  (1.4), 2
utilitarian framework in extreme
  practice settings, (8.4), 33

## V

values
  articulation and assertion of,
    (9.1), 35
  conscientious objection and, 21
  defined, 46
  integrity and, (5.4), 20–21
  integrity of profession and, (9.2),
    35–36
  nursing, promotion of (Provision 9),
    35–37
  social justice in nursing and health
    policy, (9.4), 36–37
  social justice integration, (9.3), 36

values *(continued)*
   wholeness of character and,
     (5.3), 20
virtue
   defined, 46
   moral, environment and, (6.1), 23

## W

war, human rights in context of, (8.4),
   33
well-being, promotion of, (5.2), 19
whistleblowers, (3.5), 12–13
wholeness of character, preservation
   of, (5.3), 20
work setting. *See also* healthcare

environment; workplace
   confidentiality in (3.1), 9
   ethical environment of (Provision
     6), 23–24
workplace. *See also* healthcare
   environment; work setting
   conflicts of interest in (2.2), 18
   impaired practice and (3.6), 13
   as morally good environment
     (6.3), 25
   responsibility for advocacy in
     (6.3), 24
World Health Organization
   (WHO), 31
World Medical Association, xii